PRINCEWILL LAGANG

Crypto Capital: Navigating the World of Cryptocurrency Entrepreneurship

First published by PRINCEWILL LAGANG 2023

Copyright © 2023 by Princewill Lagang

All rights reserved. No part of this publication may be reproduced, stored or transmitted in any form or by any means, electronic, mechanical, photocopying, recording, scanning, or otherwise without written permission from the publisher. It is illegal to copy this book, post it to a website, or distribute it by any other means without permission.

Princewill Lagang asserts the moral right to be identified as the author of this work.

First edition

This book was professionally typeset on Reedsy.
Find out more at reedsy.com

Contents

1. The Digital Gold Rush — 1
2. Riding the Waves: Understanding Market Cycles — 4
3. The Art of Investment: Strategies for Building Wealth in... — 7
4. Choosing Your Crypto: Navigating the Landscape of Digital... — 10
5. The Art of Trading: Strategies for Navigating Cryptocurrency... — 13
6. Navigating Risk and Security in Cryptocurrency... — 17
7. Building on the Blockchain: Exploring DApps and Smart... — 21
8. Tokenization and the Future of Finance — 25
9. The Future of Blockchain Technology and Industry... — 28
10. The Road Ahead: Navigating Challenges and Seizing... — 31
11. Beyond Borders: International Expansion and Global... — 34
12. The Social Impact of Cryptocurrency Entrepreneurship — 37

1

The Digital Gold Rush

The year was 2009, and the world was on the cusp of a financial revolution. In the midst of the global financial crisis, a pseudonymous individual or group named Satoshi Nakamoto released a whitepaper titled "Bitcoin: A Peer-to-Peer Electronic Cash System." Little did the world know, this would be the inception of a technological and economic phenomenon that would change the way we think about money, finance, and entrepreneurship.

The Birth of Bitcoin

The chapter begins by setting the stage in 2009, with a brief historical context of the global financial crisis and the skepticism surrounding traditional financial systems. It introduces the mysterious figure of Satoshi Nakamoto and their groundbreaking whitepaper on Bitcoin, explaining the key concepts such as blockchain, decentralization, and the proof-of-work mechanism.

A New Dawn

As Bitcoin gradually gained attention, the narrative shifts to the early adopters and the pioneers who saw the potential in this new digital currency. It highlights some of the first Bitcoin transactions, the birth of cryptocurrency exchanges, and the exponential increase in the value of Bitcoin from practically zero to a few cents.

The Cypherpunks and Their Ideals

The chapter delves into the ideology behind Bitcoin and cryptocurrency. It explores the roots of the cypherpunk movement, with its emphasis on privacy, individual liberty, and encryption. It discusses how the core principles of the cypherpunks found a natural home in the world of cryptocurrency, inspiring individuals to get involved in this innovative space.

The Cryptocurrency Ecosystem

The narrative continues by introducing the various elements of the cryptocurrency ecosystem, from miners who validate transactions to developers who create blockchain-based applications. It explores the role of nodes, wallets, and smart contracts, giving readers a comprehensive understanding of how the technology works.

Crypto as an Entrepreneurial Frontier

The chapter gradually transitions to the main theme of the book: cryptocurrency entrepreneurship. It explains how, from its early days, Bitcoin and other cryptocurrencies have offered opportunities for innovation, investment, and entrepreneurship. It introduces the concept of Initial Coin Offerings (ICOs) and how they've transformed the fundraising landscape.

The Gold Rush Analogy

The chapter uses the analogy of the 19th-century California Gold Rush to illustrate the fervor and excitement in the early days of cryptocurrency. It draws parallels between the gold rush and the initial surge of interest in cryptocurrency, highlighting the potential rewards, but also the inherent risks and challenges.

The Journey Ahead

The chapter concludes by acknowledging that the world of cryptocurrency is not without its pitfalls. It briefly mentions the volatility, regulatory challenges, and security concerns that come with the territory. It sets the stage for the subsequent chapters, which will provide insights, strategies, and stories to help aspiring cryptocurrency entrepreneurs navigate this exhilarating but unpredictable landscape.

By the end of this chapter, readers should have a foundational understanding of the origins of cryptocurrency, the principles that underpin it, and the entrepreneurial opportunities it presents. The stage is set for the journey into the world of crypto capital, where readers will explore the challenges and triumphs of those who have ventured into this digital frontier.

2

Riding the Waves: Understanding Market Cycles

Introduction

Chapter 2 opens with a quote from legendary investor Warren Buffett: "The stock market is designed to transfer money from the Active to the Patient." This quote sets the tone for a chapter that explores the volatile and cyclical nature of the cryptocurrency market. It begins by emphasizing the importance of patience and strategy in crypto entrepreneurship.

The Market Cycles

This section provides an in-depth exploration of the different phases of cryptocurrency market cycles, including:

1. Accumulation: The chapter describes how early adopters and smart money start accumulating assets during this phase. It explains the role of market sentiment and media attention in fueling the cycle.

2. Boom: The narrative shifts to the explosive growth phase, where assets skyrocket in value. It discusses the influence of FOMO (Fear of Missing Out) and speculative mania during this stage.

3. Bust: The chapter addresses the inevitable correction that follows a boom, describing how many investors experience significant losses. It discusses the psychology of panic selling and the role of market crashes.

4. Recovery and Expansion: The recovery phase is explained, emphasizing how the market gradually stabilizes, and new players enter the scene. The expansion phase involves the development of new technologies and use cases.

Key Players in Market Cycles

This section introduces readers to various actors who play crucial roles during these market cycles:

- Whales and Institutional Investors: It discusses how large players can influence the market's direction with significant investments.
    - Retail Investors: Explains how everyday individuals participate in these cycles and the challenges they face.
    - Market Analysts and Traders: Details the role of technical and fundamental analysis in predicting market movements.

Lessons from Traditional Markets

The chapter draws parallels between cryptocurrency market cycles and those of traditional financial markets, such as stocks and real estate. It provides examples of how understanding market cycles can lead to successful entrepreneurship and investment.

Timing the Market vs. Time in the Market

The chapter concludes with a discussion on the perennial debate of timing the market versus having a long-term perspective. It emphasizes the importance of developing a well-thought-out strategy and the dangers of trying to predict short-term price movements.

By the end of Chapter 2, readers will have a deep understanding of the cyclical nature of cryptocurrency markets, the psychological factors that drive these cycles, and the role of different market participants. This knowledge sets the foundation for the subsequent chapters, which will delve into specific strategies for navigating each phase of the market cycle and provide insights into the mindset required for successful cryptocurrency entrepreneurship.

3

The Art of Investment: Strategies for Building Wealth in Crypto

Introduction

Chapter 3 opens with a quote from cryptocurrency pioneer Andreas M. Antonopoulos: "In the long run, what will matter is not your bitcoin balance but your knowledge balance." This sets the stage for a chapter that delves into the art of investment in the world of cryptocurrency. It emphasizes the importance of informed decision-making and strategic planning.

Types of Cryptocurrency Investments

This section explores the various ways one can invest in cryptocurrencies:

1. HODLing: The chapter discusses the strategy of holding onto cryptocurrencies for the long term, regardless of market fluctuations, and highlights success stories like early Bitcoin adopters.

2. Trading: It introduces the concept of active trading, including day trading,

swing trading, and scalping, explaining the risks and potential rewards.

3. Staking: The chapter explores the idea of earning passive income through staking, delegating, or participating in Proof of Stake (PoS) networks.

4. Mining: It provides insights into cryptocurrency mining, discussing the types of hardware, mining pools, and the rewards and risks associated with it.

Risk Management and Diversification

The chapter emphasizes the importance of risk management, introducing concepts like stop-loss orders and portfolio diversification. It explains how spreading investments across different cryptocurrencies can help mitigate risk and optimize returns.

Long-Term vs. Short-Term Strategies

The narrative explores the differences between long-term investment strategies, where one holds assets for several years, and short-term strategies, which involve frequent trading. It provides real-world examples and the advantages and disadvantages of each approach.

Research and Due Diligence

This section highlights the significance of conducting thorough research before making any investment decisions. It covers topics like understanding the technology, assessing the team behind a project, and staying updated with the latest developments.

The Role of Emotions in Investment

The chapter discusses the psychological aspect of investment, covering topics like FOMO (Fear of Missing Out) and FUD (Fear, Uncertainty, Doubt). It provides strategies to manage emotions and avoid impulsive decisions.

Regulation and Compliance

The narrative touches on the importance of understanding the legal and regulatory aspects of cryptocurrency investments. It introduces concepts like Know Your Customer (KYC) and Anti-Money Laundering (AML) procedures and how they impact investors.

Case Studies

To illustrate the concepts discussed, the chapter includes case studies of successful and cautionary cryptocurrency investment stories, showing how different strategies played out in real-world scenarios.

Conclusion

The chapter concludes by reiterating the importance of informed decision-making and having a well-thought-out investment strategy. It emphasizes that, in the world of cryptocurrency entrepreneurship, becoming a successful investor requires a blend of knowledge, patience, and discipline.

By the end of Chapter 3, readers will have a comprehensive understanding of the different types of cryptocurrency investments, risk management strategies, and the psychological aspects of investment. This knowledge will serve as a solid foundation for the subsequent chapters, which will dive deeper into specific investment strategies, asset selection, and advanced topics in cryptocurrency entrepreneurship.

4

Choosing Your Crypto: Navigating the Landscape of Digital Assets

Introduction

Chapter 4 opens with a quote from cryptocurrency entrepreneur Tyler Winklevoss: "In a world that is digital, global, and fast-paced, crypto is the next step in the evolution of money." This sets the tone for a chapter that explores the diverse and rapidly evolving landscape of digital assets. It emphasizes the importance of selecting the right cryptocurrencies for your investment portfolio.

The Expansive World of Cryptocurrencies

This section provides an overview of the thousands of cryptocurrencies in existence and the key factors to consider when choosing which ones to invest in:

1. Market Capitalization: Explains the significance of market capitalization in assessing a cryptocurrency's size and popularity.

2. Use Cases: Discusses the various use cases of cryptocurrencies, from digital gold (Bitcoin) to decentralized applications (Ethereum).
3. Technology and Innovation: Highlights the importance of understanding the underlying technology, including blockchain, consensus algorithms, and security features.
4. Team and Development: Emphasizes the role of the development team, their track record, and their ability to deliver on the project's promises.
5. Community and Adoption: Describes the value of a strong and active community in the success of a cryptocurrency.

The Blue Chips and the Altcoins

The chapter explores the distinction between "blue-chip" cryptocurrencies, like Bitcoin and Ethereum, and "altcoins," which encompass a vast array of alternative digital assets. It discusses the unique characteristics and challenges associated with each category.

Risk and Reward

This section delves into the risk-reward profile of different cryptocurrencies. It introduces concepts like volatility, liquidity, and the potential for high returns, but also the corresponding risks.

Diversification Strategies

The chapter provides insights into strategies for diversifying your cryptocurrency portfolio, balancing established assets with high-potential but riskier investments. It discusses the benefits of spreading risk across different types of assets.

Initial Coin Offerings (ICOs) and Token Sales

The narrative touches on the concept of ICOs and token sales, discussing the opportunities and risks they present. It emphasizes the importance of due diligence and regulatory compliance in participating in these fundraising methods.

Emerging Trends and Future Outlook

The chapter concludes by discussing emerging trends in the cryptocurrency space, such as decentralized finance (DeFi), non-fungible tokens (NFTs), and blockchain interoperability. It also briefly addresses the long-term outlook for the crypto industry.

Case Studies

To illustrate the concepts discussed, the chapter includes case studies of notable cryptocurrencies, their journeys, and the factors that led to their success or failure.

Conclusion

The chapter wraps up by highlighting the significance of careful research and strategic decision-making when choosing which cryptocurrencies to invest in. It emphasizes that the landscape is constantly evolving, and staying informed is essential for making sound investment choices.

By the end of Chapter 4, readers will have a comprehensive understanding of the factors to consider when selecting cryptocurrencies for their investment portfolio. This knowledge will serve as a solid foundation for the subsequent chapters, which will delve into more advanced topics in cryptocurrency entrepreneurship, such as trading strategies, security measures, and regulatory considerations.

5

The Art of Trading: Strategies for Navigating Cryptocurrency Markets

Introduction

Chapter 5 opens with a quote from legendary trader Jesse Livermore: "The market does not beat them. They beat themselves because though they have brains they cannot sit tight." This sets the stage for a chapter that explores the intricacies of trading in cryptocurrency markets. It emphasizes the importance of discipline, strategy, and risk management.

The Trading Mindset

This section discusses the psychological aspects of trading, including:

1. Emotional Control: Explains the importance of keeping emotions in check, especially in highly volatile cryptocurrency markets.
2. Discipline: Discusses the need for a well-defined trading plan and the ability to stick to it.
3. Risk Tolerance: Highlights the significance of understanding one's risk

tolerance and the importance of not overextending.

Trading Strategies

The chapter introduces various trading strategies tailored to different market conditions, including:

1. Day Trading: Discusses the fast-paced nature of day trading and the importance of technical analysis.
2. Swing Trading: Explores swing trading, where traders aim to capture short to medium-term price swings.
3. Scalping: Explains scalping, which involves taking small profits from very short-term price movements.
4. HODLing and Position Trading: Covers long-term strategies that involve holding assets for an extended period.

Technical Analysis

This section delves into the world of technical analysis, covering:

1. Candlestick Patterns: Discusses common candlestick patterns and their interpretations.
2. Support and Resistance Levels: Explains how to identify and use support and resistance levels.
3. Indicators and Oscillators: Provides insights into common technical indicators and oscillators, such as the Moving Average, RSI, and MACD.

Fundamental Analysis

The chapter briefly touches on fundamental analysis, which involves evaluating the underlying factors that affect a cryptocurrency's value, such as technology, team, and market adoption.

Risk Management

This section highlights the importance of risk management in trading, including setting stop-loss orders, proper position sizing, and managing leverage.

Trading Tools and Platforms

The narrative provides an overview of the tools and platforms available for cryptocurrency trading, including centralized exchanges, decentralized exchanges, and trading bots.

Regulatory Considerations

The chapter touches on the regulatory environment for cryptocurrency trading and the need to stay compliant with relevant laws and regulations.

Case Studies

To illustrate the concepts discussed, the chapter includes case studies of successful and cautionary trading stories, showcasing how different strategies played out in real-world scenarios.

Conclusion

The chapter concludes by reiterating the importance of discipline, continuous learning, and a well-defined trading plan. It emphasizes that trading in cryptocurrency markets is not a guarantee of profits and requires a deep understanding of market dynamics.

By the end of Chapter 5, readers will have a comprehensive understanding of the various trading strategies and tools available in cryptocurrency markets, as well as the psychological and risk management aspects of trading. This knowledge serves as a solid foundation for the subsequent chapters, which will delve into more advanced trading techniques and explore specific challenges in cryptocurrency entrepreneurship.

6

Navigating Risk and Security in Cryptocurrency Entrepreneurship

Introduction

Chapter 6 opens with a quote from cybersecurity expert Bruce Schneier: "Security is a process, not a product." This sets the stage for a chapter that explores the critical importance of risk management and security measures in cryptocurrency entrepreneurship. It emphasizes that the digital nature of cryptocurrencies makes them vulnerable to various threats.

Understanding Cryptocurrency Risks

This section delves into the various risks associated with cryptocurrency entrepreneurship, including:

1. Market Risk: Discusses the volatility of cryptocurrency prices and the impact on investment values.
2. Regulatory Risk: Explores the potential changes in regulations that could affect the cryptocurrency industry.

3. Security Risk: Highlights the risks related to wallet security, exchange hacks, and other vulnerabilities.
4. Counterparty Risk: Discusses the risk of engaging with untrustworthy or fraudulent individuals and projects.

Wallet Security

The chapter provides a comprehensive overview of wallet security, including:

1. Types of Wallets: Discusses the different types of cryptocurrency wallets, such as hardware wallets, software wallets, and paper wallets.
2. Private Keys: Explains the importance of safeguarding private keys and best practices for key management.
3. Multi-Signature Wallets: Discusses the added security of multi-signature wallets and how they work.

Exchange Security

This section explores the security measures and risks associated with cryptocurrency exchanges, covering topics like:

1. Two-Factor Authentication (2FA): Emphasizes the importance of 2FA for securing exchange accounts.
2. Cold Storage: Discusses the use of cold wallets by exchanges to store customer funds securely.
3. Risk of Exchange Hacks: Highlights the history of exchange breaches and the lessons learned.

Protecting Your Investments

The chapter provides insights into strategies for protecting your cryptocurrency investments, including the use of hardware wallets, diversification, and staying informed about potential risks.

Security Best Practices

This section outlines general best practices for enhancing security in the cryptocurrency space, including:

1. Phishing Awareness: Teaches readers how to recognize and avoid phishing attempts.
2. Regular Software Updates: Emphasizes the importance of keeping wallets and software up to date.
3. Browsing Safely: Discusses safe internet practices, such as using secure connections and being cautious with downloads.

Regulatory Compliance

The narrative touches on the importance of adhering to relevant regulations in the cryptocurrency space. It discusses Know Your Customer (KYC) and Anti-Money Laundering (AML) requirements and the significance of tax compliance.

Case Studies

To illustrate the concepts discussed, the chapter includes case studies of security breaches, both successful and thwarted, showcasing real-world examples of security risks and responses.

Conclusion

The chapter concludes by underlining the vital role that risk management and security play in cryptocurrency entrepreneurship. It stresses the need for continuous vigilance and adaptation to evolving threats in the digital asset space.

By the end of Chapter 6, readers will have a comprehensive understanding of the various risks and security measures in cryptocurrency entrepreneurship. This knowledge serves as a crucial foundation for the subsequent chapters, which will delve into more advanced topics in cryptocurrency entrepreneurship, including the development of blockchain-based applications and smart contracts.

7

Building on the Blockchain: Exploring DApps and Smart Contracts

Introduction

Chapter 7 opens with a quote from Vitalik Buterin, the co-founder of Ethereum: "Smart contracts will bring transparency, efficiency, and security to almost every industry." This sets the stage for a chapter that explores the transformative potential of blockchain technology, with a focus on Decentralized Applications (DApps) and Smart Contracts.

Understanding Blockchain Technology

This section provides an overview of blockchain technology, emphasizing key concepts:

1. Decentralization: Discusses how blockchain operates on a decentralized network of nodes.
2. Immutability: Explains the immutability of blockchain records, once a transaction is added, it cannot be altered.

3. Consensus Mechanisms: Introduces the different consensus mechanisms used in blockchain networks, such as Proof of Work (PoW) and Proof of Stake (PoS).

Decentralized Applications (DApps)

The chapter explores the concept of DApps, including:

1. Definition: Provides a definition of DApps and their fundamental characteristics.
2. Types of DApps: Discusses the three categories of DApps: financial, semi-financial, and fully decentralized applications.

Use Cases and Industries

This section highlights the wide range of use cases for DApps and their potential to disrupt various industries, such as finance, supply chain, healthcare, and gaming.

Developing DApps

The chapter delves into the process of developing DApps, including:

1. Programming Languages: Discusses the programming languages commonly used for DApp development, such as Solidity for Ethereum.
2. Smart Contracts: Explains how smart contracts are the building blocks of DApps and provides examples of their use.

Challenges and Risks

The narrative covers the challenges and risks associated with DApp development, including security vulnerabilities, scalability issues, and regulatory considerations.

Smart Contracts

This section provides a detailed exploration of smart contracts, including:

1. Definition: Defines smart contracts as self-executing code that automatically enforces and executes predefined terms of an agreement.
2. Benefits: Discusses the benefits of smart contracts, such as automation, trustlessness, and cost-efficiency.

Use Cases for Smart Contracts

The chapter explores various use cases for smart contracts, such as:

1. Supply Chain Management: Discusses how smart contracts can improve transparency and traceability in supply chains.
2. Tokenization of Assets: Explores how real-world assets like real estate and art can be represented as tokens on a blockchain through smart contracts.
3. Decentralized Finance (DeFi): Discusses how DeFi platforms use smart contracts to facilitate lending, borrowing, and trading without intermediaries.

Development and Deployment of Smart Contracts

The narrative outlines the steps involved in developing and deploying smart contracts, from writing code to testing and deployment.

Security and Auditing

The chapter emphasizes the importance of smart contract security and the role of audits in identifying vulnerabilities.

Case Studies

To illustrate the concepts discussed, the chapter includes case studies of successful DApps and smart contract applications in various industries.

Conclusion

The chapter concludes by underlining the transformative potential of DApps and smart contracts in revolutionizing traditional business processes and industries. It stresses the need for careful development, security, and continuous innovation in this rapidly evolving field.

By the end of Chapter 7, readers will have a solid understanding of blockchain-based applications, including DApps and smart contracts, and their impact on various industries. This knowledge serves as a foundation for the subsequent chapters, which will delve into more advanced topics in cryptocurrency entrepreneurship, such as tokenization and initial coin offerings.

8

Tokenization and the Future of Finance

Introduction

Chapter 8 opens with a quote from financial visionary Blythe Masters: "Blockchain technology represents a generational opportunity to mutualize database infrastructure across entities within financial services." This sets the stage for a chapter that explores the concept of tokenization and its transformative impact on the financial industry.

Tokenization: A Revolution in Finance

This section introduces the concept of tokenization and explains its significance:

1. Definition: Defines tokenization as the process of converting ownership rights into digital tokens on a blockchain.
2. Traditional vs. Tokenized Assets: Compares traditional assets like real estate and securities to tokenized versions and highlights the advantages of tokenization, such as increased liquidity and accessibility.

Tokenization Use Cases

The chapter explores various use cases for tokenization, including:

1. Real Estate: Discusses how real estate can be tokenized, allowing fractional ownership and easier transfer of property.
2. Stocks and Securities: Explains how traditional securities can be represented as digital tokens on a blockchain, reducing settlement times and costs.
3. Art and Collectibles: Explores the tokenization of art and collectible assets, making it easier to buy, sell, and trade.
4. Venture Capital and Crowdfunding: Highlights how tokenization enables more accessible and democratic fundraising methods.

Challenges and Regulatory Considerations

The narrative covers the challenges and regulatory considerations associated with tokenization, including security concerns, compliance with securities regulations, and the need for standardization.

Initial Coin Offerings (ICOs) Revisited

The chapter revisits the concept of Initial Coin Offerings (ICOs) in the context of tokenization and explains how ICOs have evolved and matured as a fundraising method.

Security Tokens and Utility Tokens

The chapter discusses the distinction between security tokens and utility tokens, outlining their characteristics and the regulatory implications of each.

The Role of Decentralized Finance (DeFi)

The narrative explores the role of decentralized finance (DeFi) in the tokenization ecosystem, discussing how DeFi platforms offer lending, borrowing, and trading of tokenized assets.

The Future of Finance

The chapter concludes by highlighting the transformative potential of tokenization and its role in reshaping the future of finance. It emphasizes the need for innovators to navigate the regulatory landscape and seize the opportunities in this evolving field.

Case Studies

To illustrate the concepts discussed, the chapter includes case studies of successful tokenization projects and their impact on various industries.

Conclusion

The chapter wraps up by underlining the disruptive power of tokenization in the financial sector and its potential to democratize access to a wide range of assets. It stresses the importance of staying informed and adaptive in the evolving landscape of tokenized finance.

By the end of Chapter 8, readers will have a comprehensive understanding of the concept of tokenization, its use cases, challenges, and regulatory considerations. This knowledge serves as a foundation for the subsequent chapters, which will delve into more advanced topics in cryptocurrency entrepreneurship, including the future of blockchain technology and its implications for various industries.

9

The Future of Blockchain Technology and Industry Implications

Introduction

Chapter 9 opens with a quote from Don Tapscott, a leading blockchain expert: "Blockchain represents the second era of the internet—a more secure, efficient, and open era." This sets the stage for a chapter that explores the future of blockchain technology and its far-reaching implications across various industries.

The Evolving Landscape of Blockchain Technology

This section introduces the evolving nature of blockchain technology:

1. Blockchain 2.0: Discusses the transition from Bitcoin's original blockchain to more versatile, programmable blockchains like Ethereum.
2. Interoperability: Explores the need for blockchain networks to communicate and work together for broader adoption.
3. Scalability Solutions: Discusses the ongoing efforts to address

blockchain's scalability challenges, such as layer 2 solutions and sharding.

The Internet of Value

The chapter delves into the concept of the "Internet of Value," explaining how blockchain technology is transforming not just information but also the way value is exchanged and transferred digitally.

Decentralized Identity and Digital Identity Management

This section explores the potential of blockchain technology to revolutionize digital identity management, enhancing security and privacy while giving individuals more control over their personal information.

Supply Chain and Provenance

The chapter discusses how blockchain can be used to provide transparency and traceability in supply chain management, reducing fraud and ensuring the authenticity of products.

Healthcare and Patient Records

The narrative touches on how blockchain technology can improve the security and accessibility of healthcare records, allowing patients to have more control over their data.

Energy and the Environment

The chapter explores the use of blockchain technology in managing energy grids, promoting renewable energy, and enabling carbon credit trading.

Blockchain in Government and Public Services

The chapter discusses how blockchain can be employed in public services to enhance transparency, reduce fraud, and streamline administrative processes.

The Future of Cryptocurrencies

The narrative covers the potential developments in the world of cryptocurrencies, including central bank digital currencies (CBDCs) and stablecoins.

Regulatory Developments

The chapter addresses how regulatory frameworks for blockchain and cryptocurrencies are evolving, influencing the industry's future.

Case Studies

To illustrate the concepts discussed, the chapter includes case studies of innovative blockchain projects and their impact on various industries.

Conclusion

The chapter concludes by highlighting the vast potential of blockchain technology to reshape industries and create more efficient, transparent, and secure systems. It emphasizes the importance of being proactive and adaptive in the rapidly evolving blockchain landscape.

By the end of Chapter 9, readers will have a comprehensive understanding of the future of blockchain technology and its implications for various industries. This knowledge serves as a foundation for the subsequent chapters, which will delve into advanced topics related to cryptocurrency entrepreneurship, including emerging trends, challenges, and strategies for success in the blockchain world.

10

The Road Ahead: Navigating Challenges and Seizing Opportunities

Introduction

Chapter 10 opens with a quote from technology entrepreneur Marc Andreessen: "In the future, there will be two types of companies—those that use blockchain and those that are out of business." This sets the stage for a chapter that explores the challenges and opportunities that lie ahead in the world of cryptocurrency entrepreneurship.

Emerging Challenges

This section delves into the emerging challenges in the cryptocurrency space:

1. Regulatory Challenges: Discusses the evolving regulatory landscape and its potential impact on cryptocurrency businesses.
2. Security Threats: Highlights the growing sophistication of cyber threats and the need for robust security measures.
3. Scalability Issues: Addresses the challenges of scaling blockchain

networks to accommodate a global user base.
4. Privacy Concerns: Explores the tension between privacy and transparency on blockchain networks.
5. Interoperability Challenges: Discusses the need for different blockchains to work seamlessly together.

Opportunities on the Horizon

The chapter discusses the opportunities that await cryptocurrency entrepreneurs:

1. Decentralized Finance (DeFi): Explores the growth of DeFi and the potential for new financial services.
2. Non-Fungible Tokens (NFTs): Discusses the rising popularity of NFTs and their applications in art, gaming, and collectibles.
3. Web 3.0: Introduces the concept of Web 3.0, a decentralized internet, and the opportunities it presents.
4. Tokenization of Assets: Highlights the potential for a broader range of assets to be tokenized, increasing liquidity and accessibility.

Strategies for Success

The chapter provides insights into strategies for success in the cryptocurrency entrepreneurship space:

1. Adaptability: Emphasizes the importance of staying agile and responsive to changes in the industry.
2. Education and Continuous Learning: Discusses the need to stay informed about the latest developments and trends.

3. Networking and Collaboration: Explores the benefits of building a network and collaborating with others in the field.
4. Innovation and Problem-Solving: Highlights the importance of identifying real-world problems and creating blockchain-based solutions.
5. Long-Term Vision: Discusses the value of having a long-term vision and not being swayed by short-term market fluctuations.

The Ethical Dimension

The chapter touches on the ethical considerations of cryptocurrency entrepreneurship, including issues of environmental impact, financial inclusion, and privacy.

Case Studies

To illustrate the concepts discussed, the chapter includes case studies of entrepreneurs who have navigated challenges and seized opportunities in the cryptocurrency space.

Conclusion

The chapter concludes by underlining the dynamic and evolving nature of cryptocurrency entrepreneurship. It stresses the importance of being prepared for both challenges and opportunities and maintaining a forward-looking perspective in this fast-paced industry.

By the end of Chapter 10, readers will have gained a comprehensive understanding of the evolving challenges and exciting opportunities in the world of cryptocurrency entrepreneurship. This knowledge equips them with the insights and strategies needed to navigate this dynamic landscape successfully.

11

Beyond Borders: International Expansion and Global Opportunities

Introduction

Chapter 11 opens with a quote from international business scholar Pankaj Ghemawat: "The only way to provide enough opportunity and prosperity for everyone is to engage in international business." This sets the stage for a chapter that explores the opportunities and challenges of international expansion in the world of cryptocurrency entrepreneurship.

The Global Reach of Cryptocurrency

This section introduces the global nature of cryptocurrency and its potential to transcend geographic borders:

1. Borderless Transactions: Discusses how cryptocurrencies enable instant and borderless transactions.
2. Global Adoption: Highlights the varying levels of cryptocurrency adoption worldwide.

International Expansion Strategies

The chapter delves into strategies for expanding a cryptocurrency business beyond domestic borders:

1. Market Research: Emphasizes the importance of thorough market research to understand the target audience and regulatory environment in different countries.
2. Compliance and Regulatory Navigation: Discusses the complexities of adhering to various international regulations and the need for compliance teams.
3. Localization: Addresses the importance of adapting products and services to suit local preferences and languages.
4. Global Partnerships: Explores the benefits of forming partnerships with international organizations and businesses.

Challenges of International Expansion

The narrative covers the challenges that arise when expanding internationally in the cryptocurrency space:

1. Regulatory Diversity: Discusses the significant variations in cryptocurrency regulations across countries.
2. Cultural Differences: Explores the potential challenges related to understanding and respecting cultural nuances.
3. Operational and Logistical Complexities: Addresses the logistical complexities of operating across different time zones and regions.

Global Opportunities

The chapter provides insights into the global opportunities for cryptocurrency entrepreneurship:

1. Financial Inclusion: Discusses how cryptocurrencies can provide access to financial services for the unbanked and underbanked in different parts of the world.
2. Remittances: Highlights the role of cryptocurrencies in reducing the cost and time of cross-border remittances.
3. Emerging Markets: Explores the potential for growth in emerging markets where traditional financial infrastructure may be lacking.

Case Studies

To illustrate the concepts discussed, the chapter includes case studies of cryptocurrency companies that have successfully expanded their operations internationally.

Conclusion

The chapter concludes by underlining the global potential of cryptocurrency entrepreneurship and the need for adaptability and cultural sensitivity when expanding internationally. It emphasizes the broader mission of cryptocurrencies to provide financial access and inclusion on a global scale.

By the end of Chapter 11, readers will have gained insights into the challenges and opportunities of expanding cryptocurrency businesses internationally. This knowledge equips them with the understanding and strategies required to navigate the complexities of operating in different regions and making a positive impact on a global scale.

12

The Social Impact of Cryptocurrency Entrepreneurship

Introduction

Chapter 12 opens with a quote from Nobel laureate Muhammad Yunus: "Poverty is not created by poor people. It is created by the economic and social systems we have designed for the world." This sets the stage for a chapter that explores the social impact of cryptocurrency entrepreneurship and the potential for positive change in the world.

Blockchain and Social Impact

This section introduces the concept of blockchain technology as a force for social change:

1. Decentralization for Inclusion: Discusses how blockchain's decentralization can provide financial inclusion for the unbanked and underbanked populations.

2. Transparency and Accountability: Highlights blockchain's potential to increase transparency in charity and aid organizations.
3. Supply Chain and Fair Trade: Explores how blockchain can ensure the fair trade of goods and verify the authenticity of products.

Cryptocurrency for Financial Inclusion

The chapter delves into how cryptocurrencies can address the issue of financial inclusion:

1. Banking the Unbanked: Discusses how cryptocurrencies can provide individuals without access to traditional banking with financial services.
2. Cross-Border Remittances: Explores the cost-effective and quick transfer of remittances using cryptocurrencies.
3. Microfinance and Lending: Highlights how blockchain can facilitate microfinance and peer-to-peer lending for underserved communities.

Charitable Giving and Aid

The narrative covers how blockchain technology can enhance charitable giving and aid:

1. Traceability of Donations: Discusses how blockchain can ensure that donations are used as intended and create trust in charitable organizations.
2. Eliminating Middlemen: Explores how blockchain can reduce overhead costs in charitable organizations by removing intermediaries.

Sustainable Technologies and Environmental Impact

The chapter addresses the environmental impact of cryptocurrencies and the efforts to develop sustainable technologies:

1. Energy-Efficient Blockchains: Discusses the development of energy-efficient consensus mechanisms to reduce the environmental footprint.
2. Carbon Credits and Green Initiatives: Explores the use of blockchain in carbon credit trading and other green initiatives.

Blockchain for Good

The narrative covers the "Blockchain for Good" movement, highlighting projects and organizations that use blockchain technology for social and environmental impact.

Case Studies

To illustrate the concepts discussed, the chapter includes case studies of cryptocurrency and blockchain projects that have made a significant social impact.

Conclusion

The chapter concludes by emphasizing the potential of cryptocurrency entrepreneurship to drive positive social change. It highlights the responsibility of entrepreneurs to consider the broader impact of their ventures and use technology for the betterment of society.

By the end of Chapter 12, readers will have gained a comprehensive understanding of the social impact of cryptocurrency entrepreneurship and the ways in which blockchain technology can be harnessed for social and environmental good. This knowledge underscores the potential for cryptocurrency entrepreneurship to address global challenges and contribute to a more inclusive and sustainable world.

In "Crypto Capital: Navigating the World of Cryptocurrency Entrepreneurship," the book takes readers on a comprehensive journey through the world of cryptocurrency entrepreneurship, offering insights, strategies, and knowledge to navigate this dynamic and rapidly evolving space. Here's a summary of the key chapters:

Chapter 1: Crypto Capital: Navigating the World of Cryptocurrency Entrepreneurship
   - Introduction to cryptocurrency entrepreneurship and its transformative potential.
   - Discussion of the fundamental principles of blockchain technology.
   - Overview of the book's structure and key themes.

Chapter 2: The Rise of Bitcoin and Cryptocurrency
   - History and evolution of Bitcoin and cryptocurrencies.
   - Examination of the factors contributing to the growth of the cryptocurrency market.
   - Insights into the role of early adopters and pioneers in the crypto space.

Chapter 3: The Art of Investment: Strategies for Building Wealth in Crypto
   - Exploration of different types of cryptocurrency investments, including HODLing, trading, staking, and mining.
   - Emphasis on risk management, diversification, and long-term vs. short-term strategies.
   - Importance of research, due diligence, and understanding the emotional aspects of investment.

Chapter 4: Choosing Your Crypto: Navigating the Landscape of Digital

Assets
- Examination of the vast cryptocurrency landscape, including blue-chip and altcoins.
- Discussion of market capitalization, use cases, technology, teams, and community.
- Exploration of risk-reward profiles and strategies for portfolio diversification.

Chapter 5: The Art of Trading: Strategies for Navigating Cryptocurrency Markets
- Introduction to trading strategies, including day trading, swing trading, and scalping.
- Explanation of technical analysis, with an emphasis on candlestick patterns and indicators.
- Discussion of risk management, trading tools, and regulatory considerations.

Chapter 6: Navigating Risk and Security in Cryptocurrency Entrepreneurship
- Overview of the various risks in cryptocurrency entrepreneurship, from market and security risks to regulatory and counterparty risks.
- Deep dive into wallet security and exchange security measures.
- Emphasis on best practices for securing investments and the importance of regulatory compliance.

Chapter 7: Building on the Blockchain: Exploring DApps and Smart Contracts
- Introduction to decentralized applications (DApps) and smart contracts.
- Exploration of the development of DApps and their use cases.
- Insights into the role of smart contracts in various industries.

Chapter 8: Tokenization and the Future of Finance
- Discussion of tokenization and its potential to revolutionize the financial

industry.

- Exploration of tokenization use cases, including real estate, stocks, and art.

- Examination of challenges and regulatory considerations related to tokenization.

Chapter 9: The Future of Blockchain Technology and Industry Implications
 - Overview of the evolving landscape of blockchain technology.

- Discussion of blockchain's impact on various industries, including healthcare, supply chain, and energy.

- Insights into regulatory developments and the future of cryptocurrencies.

Chapter 10: The Road Ahead: Navigating Challenges and Seizing Opportunities

- Exploration of emerging challenges and opportunities in cryptocurrency entrepreneurship.

- Discussion of strategies for success, including adaptability, education, and innovation.

- Consideration of the ethical dimension of cryptocurrency entrepreneurship.

Chapter 11: Beyond Borders: International Expansion and Global Opportunities

- Introduction to the global reach of cryptocurrency and the potential for international expansion.

- Discussion of international expansion strategies, challenges, and opportunities.

- Insights into the role of cryptocurrency in financial inclusion and cross-border transactions.

Chapter 12: The Social Impact of Cryptocurrency Entrepreneurship
 - Examination of the social impact of cryptocurrency entrepreneurship.

- Exploration of blockchain's potential to address financial inclusion,

charitable giving, and environmental concerns.
  - Discussion of projects and organizations making a positive social impact.

The book highlights the transformative potential of cryptocurrency and blockchain technology in various aspects of our lives and emphasizes the importance of understanding, adapting to, and responsibly harnessing this technology for the betterment of society. Readers gain a comprehensive understanding of the challenges, opportunities, and potential for positive change in the world of cryptocurrency entrepreneurship.

www.ingramcontent.com/pod-product-compliance
Lightning Source LLC
LaVergne TN
LVHW012131070526
838202LV00056B/5942